BONNARD

POSTERS AND LITHOGRAPH

THE LITTLE LIBRARY
OF ART

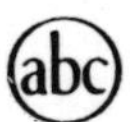

BONNARD

POSTERS AND LITHOGRAPHS

BY

ANTOINE TERRASSE

METHUEN AND CO LTD

11 NEW FETTER LANE · LONDON EC4

TUDOR PUBLISHING CO.

NEW YORK

ACHEVÉ D'IMPRIMER EN MAI 1970
PAR CITÉ-PRESS, PARIS
CLICHÉS PERROT ET GRISET, PARIS

"The first poster print to explode gaily over the walls of Paris since the time of Daumier was *France Champagne,* the work of Bonnard, which is unobtainable today. It was quite different from Chéret's charming, mural illuminations and gave a fresh impetus to the art of lithography, which Toulouse-Lautrec, its acknowledged master, developed with such an incomparable subtlety." Octave Mirbeau, in these words taken from his Preface to the Catalogue of the Sale of the Thadée Natanson Collection in 1908, emphasised the importance of Pierre Bonnard's contribution to lithography when he designed this poster.

Experiments in the process of colour lithography had been carried out since the early part of the 19th century, but did not achieve really satisfactory results until the poster-designer Jules Chéret thought of applying it to posters. Many of the countless designs he produced had an exceptional charm, but *France Champagne* suggested fresh possibilities in a style of skilful ingenuousness; the composition was unusual, the distortions of the drawing

daring, printer's characters contrasted with rounded letters traced with a brush, and the distribution of black on a coloured background was unusual. As soon as it was pasted on the walls at the end of March 1891, Toulouse-Lautrec decided to design posters himself. Bonnard took him to his printer, Ancourt, but when he recognised Lautrec's genius, he left, or almost left the field free to him; during a career that was in other respects longer than Lautrec's, he only designed nine posters after *France Champagne*. These were:
La Revue Blanche (1894), *Les Peintres-Graveurs* (June 1896), *Le Salon des Cent* (August 1896), *L'Estampe et l'Affiche* (1897), *Le Figaro* (March 1903), *Le Figaro* (Small poster, 1903), *Le Salon d'Automne* (1912), *Les Ballets Russes* ("La Légende de Joseph", May 1914), *Le Bulletin de la Vie Artistique* (December 1919) [See Note 1]. Yet Bonnard never gave up lithography and often returned to it until the end of his life. This was not only because the flexibility of the technique appealed to his artistic temperament, it also brought an element of change into his work, which was indispensable to him. His enquiring, exacting mind felt the need to experiment in several directions and apply what he had learnt from one to another. He worked with different techniques simultaneously just as he used to work on several paintings at the same time. "I have learnt a great deal about painting from doing coloured lithographs. You can discover a great many things by having to study tonal relationships when there are only four or five colours to play with, super-

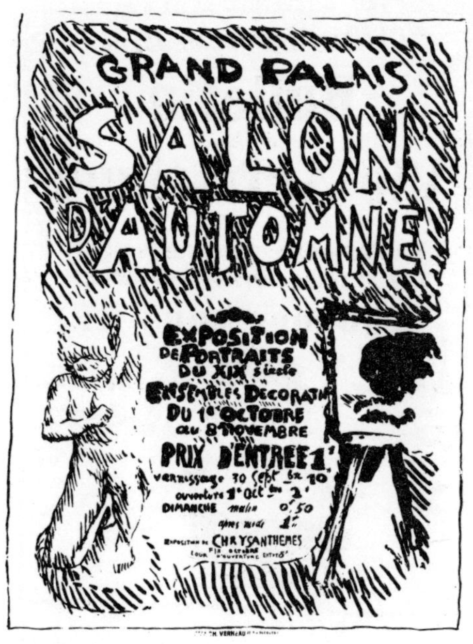

POSTER FOR THE SALON D'AUTOMNE IN 1912.

impose or juxtapose." The size of a collection
of prints, the format of a book, even the process
of lithography imposes a certain discipline and,
although they did not confine him to a strict
rule, which his imagination would never have
accepted, they did at least require more control.
After he had done the illustrations for *Petites*

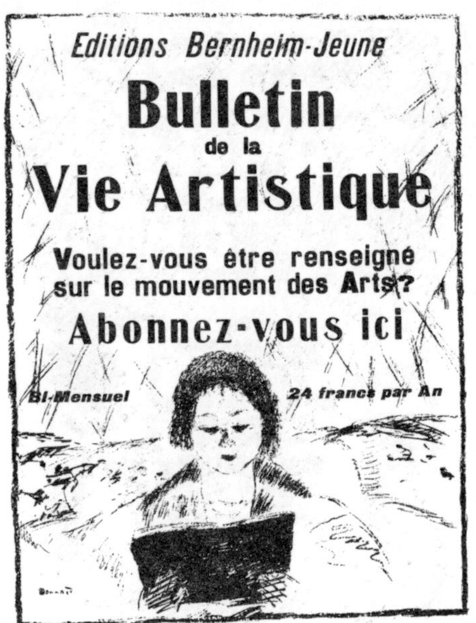

POSTER FOR "LE BULLETIN DE LA VIE
ARTISTIQUE". DECEMBER 1919.

Scènes Familières, prints for various illustrated
books, the series of *Quelques Aspects de la Vie
de Paris,* the illustrations for Verlaine's *Parallèlement* and Longus's *Daphnis and Chloë,* there was
a marked change in the style of his painting
towards a more assured composition.

We, who have the simpler task of looking at

them, can enjoy the charm of Bonnard's spontaneous sensibility with its mixture of irony and tenderness. As we look at each vignette of life in a Paris that has disappeared, the flavour of a time regained returns, a flavour that without Bonnard would have been lost completely.

*

Plate 1: FRANCE CHAMPAGNE. 1891. Poster. After Octave Mirbeau, Francis Jourdain and Thadée Natanson described in their memories of Bonnard the surprise they felt when they saw this poster. "I should like to trace back to his beginnings the young artist of this poster, which opened a new world to me. Yes, a new world, whose existence was confirmed for me a few weeks later by another poster, introducing Parisians to the *Bal du Moulin Rouge* and also signed by an unknown name, Lautrec. These two designs had little in common, nothing, in fact, but their audacity, which created a sort of relationship between them—audacity and novelty . . ." (Francis Jourdain, *Le Point,* No. XXIV, 1943). Bonnard himself was both surprised and delighted by his success. "Everyone's asking for my poster. Coquelin Cadet, who knows one of my friends, has asked me for one. I have also designed the cover of a book of music for the gentleman of the Champagne poster for which he has paid me 40 francs !" (Letter to his mother, 21 May 1891) [See Note 2].

Plate 2: FAMILY SCENE. 1893. Lithograph.
In a review of the Salon des Indépendants, as early as 1892, Felix Fénéon had described Bonnard as "very Japanesy". The influence of Japanese prints is especially noticeable here. One detail, in particular, the squares on the fabric, drawn flat, attracts the eye. The harmony of the colours is set off by the dark areas, which strengthen the visual effect of the whole. A final Japanese touch can be seen in the figures in close-up against a monochrome background.

Plate 3: DOGS. 1893. Lithograph.
None of the absorbing occupations of dogs escaped Bonnard. Very "busy about their own business", they take not the slightest notice of the poor carriage hack, which reappears on the frieze of a lithographic screen (See pl. 5). The vitality of the drawing is extraordinary. A few strokes thrown onto the paper and livened by a deep, black patch slightly off centre . . .

Plate 4: LA REVUE BLANCHE. 1894. Poster.
Thadée Natanson, who had been attracted very early on by the works of Bonnard, all the Nabis and Toulouse-Lautrec at the Galerie Le Barc de Boutteville, was the founder and editor of the *Revue Blanche*. He asked Bonnard in 1894 and Lautrec in 1895 to design a poster for this avant-garde literary review, which for the twelve years of its existence counted the greatest writers and artists of the day among its contributors. The grey, beige and pinkish

browns accented with black of Bonnard's poster are a delicate evocation of the colours of the city in winter. Only the face of the chilly passer-by in the centre can be seen clearly, like the "negative of a wolf" (Robert Delevoy). The letters of the words *Revue Blanche,* standing out in white, beat the insistant rhythm of an irrestible dance of little reviews, which already covered the walls of Paris.

Plate 5:   NURSEMAIDS OUT FOR A WALK: FRIEZE OF CARRIAGES (Screen of four sheets of paper). 1899.   Lithograph.
The composition of the screen falls into three distinct parts.   The first comprises the frieze of waiting carriages in the upper part of the four sheets; the second is a group of three young women walking towards a little balustrade on the two sheets to the left; the third is formed by the figures of a woman and children running right over the two sheets to the right. The three parts are linked by the frieze itself and the movement of a hoop, which repeats the circles of the carriage wheels.   This arrangement and certain other features, like the accents of black, the silent spaces of white, the avoidance of symmetry and the different designs on the fabrics, are reminiscent of some Japanese prints. Not a single carriage is quite like another and he has even drawn in some of the coachmen. The colours are very equally balanced in spite of their imbalance and the striped blue of a cape, like staves of music, makes the whole print sing.

Plate 6: WOMAN WITH AN UMBRELLA. 1895.
Lithograph.
This lithograph was published in 1895 by the
Revue Blanche in a collection of lithographs by
Lautrec, Bonnard, Vuillard and Roussel. The
outline of a fragile figure steps into a luminous
space with infinite care. A faint flush on her
face betrays her emotion, but she is not alone;
behind her, the monogram PB flutters like a
butterfly.

Plate 7: THE LITTLE LAUNDRESS. 1896. Lithograph.
Although several sketches taken from life and
one preliminary water-colour exist of this
subject—this was Bonnard's usual practice—the
freshness of the first sketch still remains in
the lithograph. It is pointless to discuss the
power of suggestion in a few touches of skil-
fully distributed colour. The little laundress
is unforgettable, once you have met her. The
print itself, which shows an exquisite sensitive-
ness—but modesty is saved by a touch of
humour—could serve as an ideogram of Bonnard's lithographic art.

Plate 8: LE SALON DES CENT. August 1896.
Poster.
The Salon des Cent was held on the premises
of the publishing house of La Plume, 31 rue
Bonaparte, where posters and prints from
countries all over the world were exhibited.
Bonnard's poster, advertising the XXIII Group

Exhibition of the Salon, has a remarkable
simplicity. .A single, unbroken line drawn in
the centre traces the profile of a young woman.
Her hair dressed in a bun, her veil, low-cut,
trailing dress and her gloved hand are drawn
with both lightness and precision, which pre-
serve a fashion for us and a fleeting moment
from the life of a woman of Paris. The letters
in blue ink are clearly spread over the background and the amusing monogram PB, like
a large seal, contributes the requisite touch of
piquancy.

Plate 9: BARROW BOY. 1899. Lithograph.
This lithograph belongs to the series *Quelques
Aspects de la Vie de Paris,* which occupied
Bonnard for a long time. A more than usually
large number of subjects correspond to those
he chose for his paintings. Ambroise Vollard
commissioned the series of twelve coloured
prints, which were published in 1899. The
black in the centre of the composition is start-
ling, but the pool of yellow light seems more
brilliant by contrast with the black and would
hardly be possible without it.

Plate 10: HOUSE IN A COURTYARD. 1899.
Lithograph.
This house in a courtyard, seen from a half-open
window, appears in four pictures of Montmartre
painted in 1895-7. The lithograph is like a
detail from one of the paintings. Bonnard
delighted in the decorative effect of the lines

of the windows, the little squares and the slatted shutters against the walls. The bare, luminous wall stands as a contrast with them, while the little red patches of the chimneys and the black openings provide accents of colour. The strength of the composition lies in the vertical lines formed by the sections of wall and by one of the stiles of the window opening onto the outside.

Plate 11: PARALLÈLEMENT. 1900. Lithograph.
The lithographs drawn in red chalk, which illustrate the poems of Verlaine, wind in and out of the printed verses and spread all over the margins. Together they form one of the finest books published by Ambroise Vollard. Bonnard was anxious to have this pinkish red tint, because it made it "easier for him to suggest the poetic atmosphere of Verlaine".

Plate 12: LE FIGARO. March 1903. Poster.

Plate 13: LE FIGARO. 1903. Small, interior poster.
Bonnard designed two posters for the *Figaro* in 1903. One was a small poster for hanging inside a house, advertising a new novel by Abel Hermant, which was going to appear in the newspaper, and a large poster. He has not played with the effects of fancy lettering as in earlier posters, but connected his design to the printer's type-face by a coloured stroke.

Plate 14: THE GRAPES. 1942. Lithograph.
This was the first of a series of lithographs
commissioned from the painter by Louis Carré.
The great colourist of the final years has left
his mark on every one of the plates, which
were transferred to stone by Jacques Villon.

Plate 15: THE BATH. 1943. Lithograph.
The bath was one of Bonnard's favourite subjects. The orange harmonies are character-
istic of his last paintings; yellow and orange
were the colours that best symbolised the light
that flooded his painting more and more in his
last years.

Note 1. — The four following sketches were not complet-
ed in a final version: *Moulin Rouge* (1891; colour repro-
duction in Charles Terrasse, *Bonnard*, Paris 1927);
Le Cri de Paris (about 1894 ; *op. cit.*, reproduced in
black and white); sketches for a *Seaside Resort in
Normandy* (about 1895; reproduced in the catalogues
to the Bonnard exhibitions at Munich, 1966, and Ham-
burg, 1970) and for the *Parfumerie Bonnard* (cf. Claude
Roger-Marx, *Bonnard*, Paris 1924).

Note 2. — For further information on this poster, the
following sources should be consulted: Charles Terrasse,
Bonnard, Paris 1927; Mme Hedy Hahnloser, *Félix Vallot-
ton et ses Amis*, Paris 1936; Claude Roger-Marx, *Bonnard
Lithographe*, Monaco, 1952; see also the note by Mme Hedy
Hahnloser, quoted in Annette Vaillant, *Bonnard*,
Neuchâtel 1965.

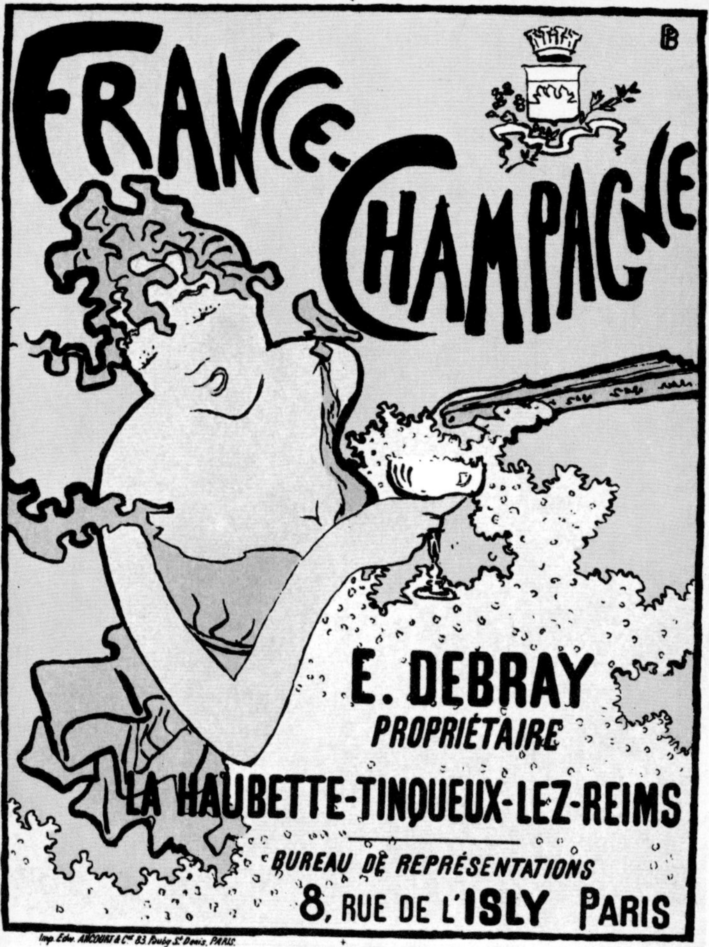

FRANCE-CHAMPAGNE
E. DEBRAY
PROPRIÉTAIRE
LA HAUBETTE-TINQUEUX-LEZ-REIMS
BUREAU DE REPRÉSENTATIONS
8, RUE DE L'ISLY PARIS
Imp. Edw. ANCOURT & Cie 83. Fbubg St Denis. PARIS.

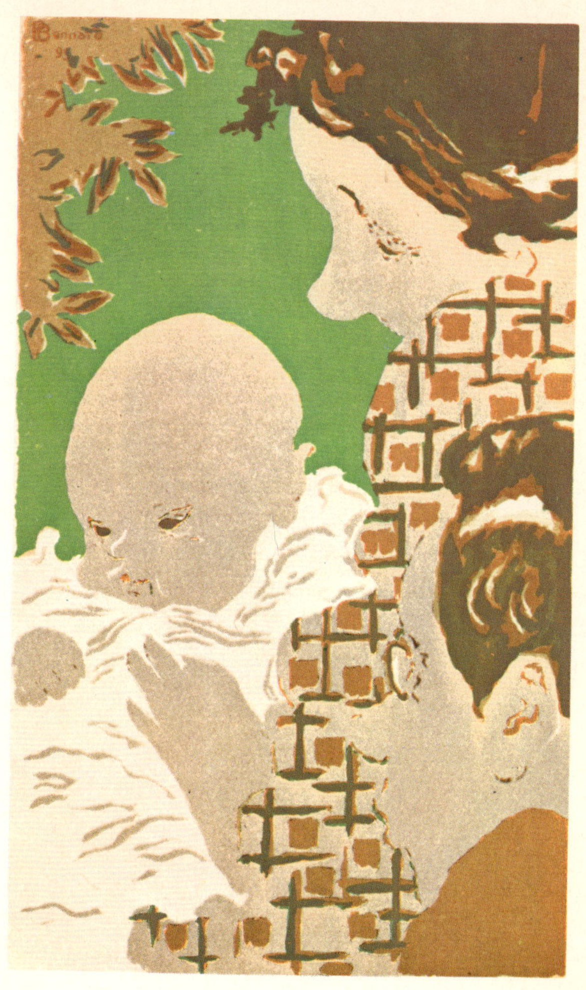

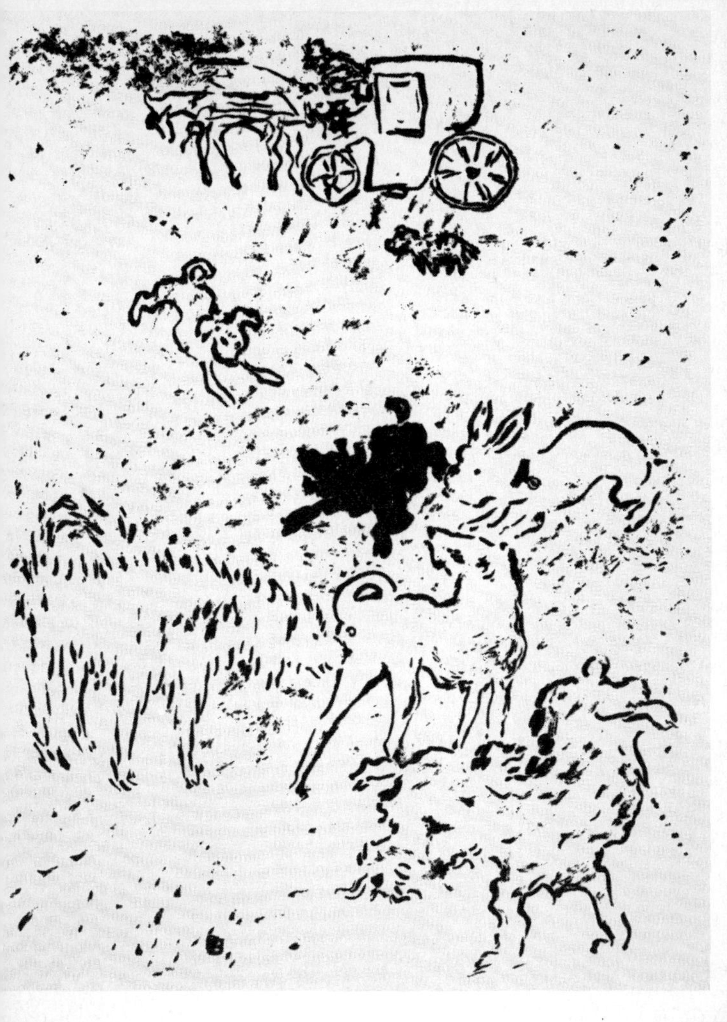

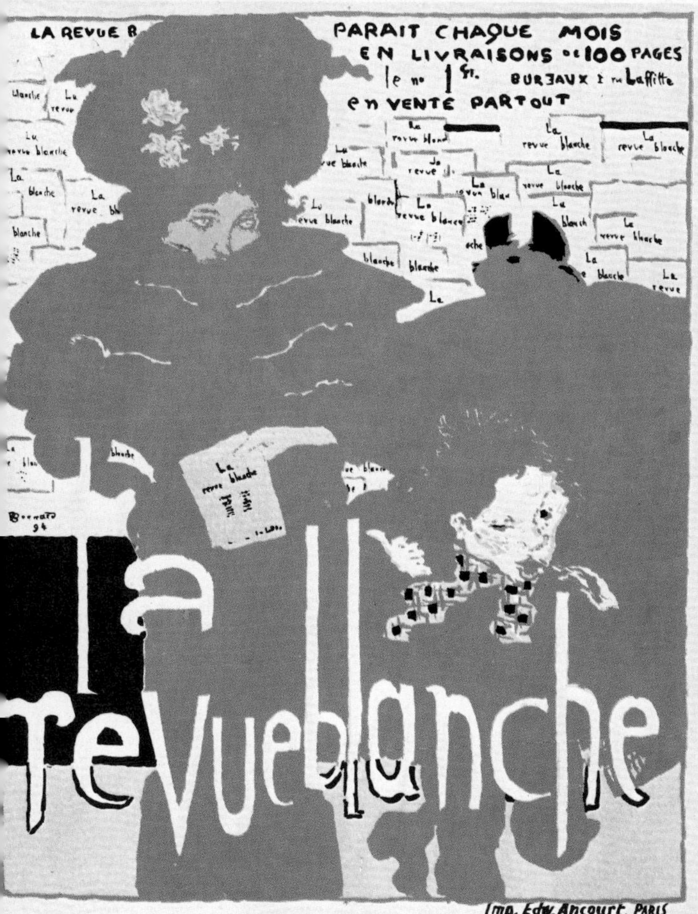

LA REVUE B
PARAIT CHAQUE MOIS
EN LIVRAISONS DE 100 PAGES
le no 1 fr. BUREAUX 1 ru Laffitte
EN VENTE PARTOUT
Bonnard 94
La revueblanche
Imp. Edw. Ancourt, PARIS

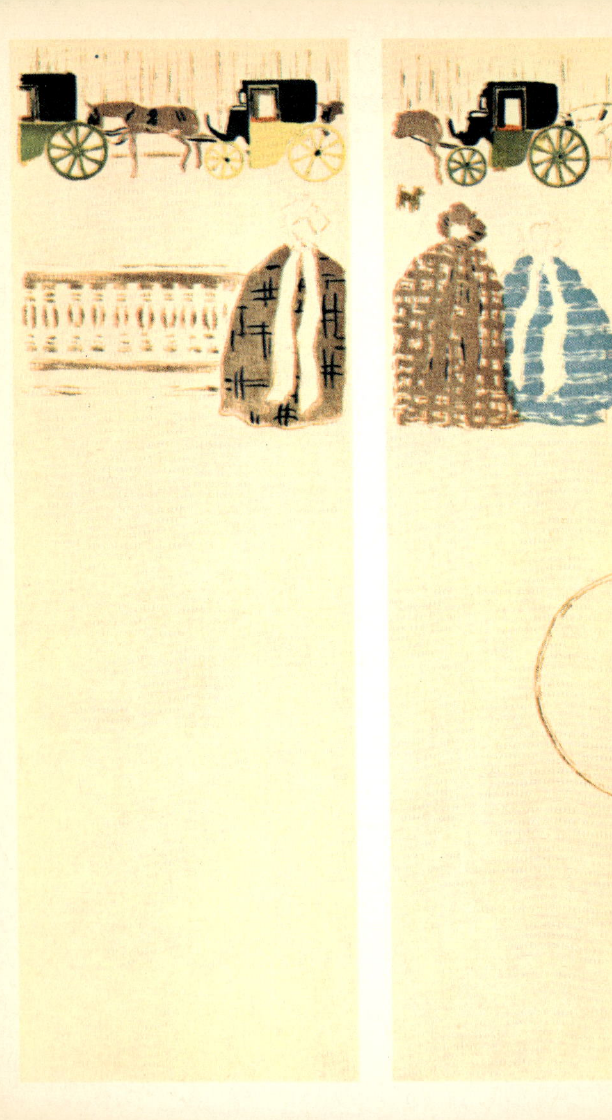

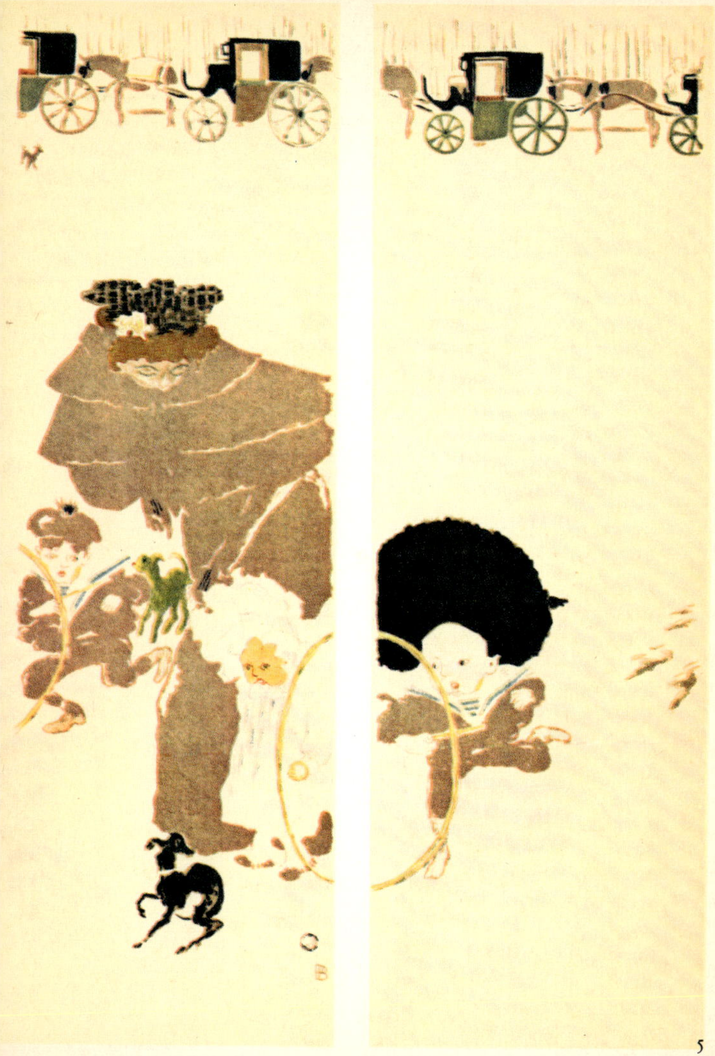

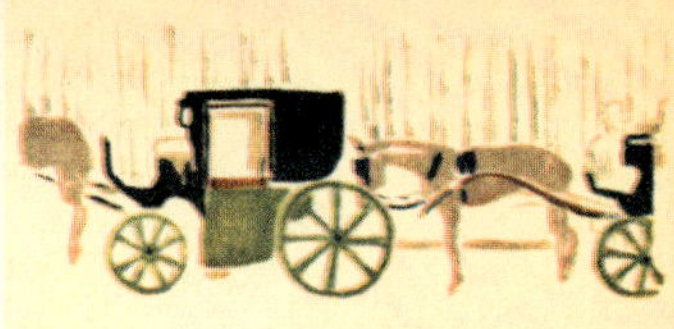

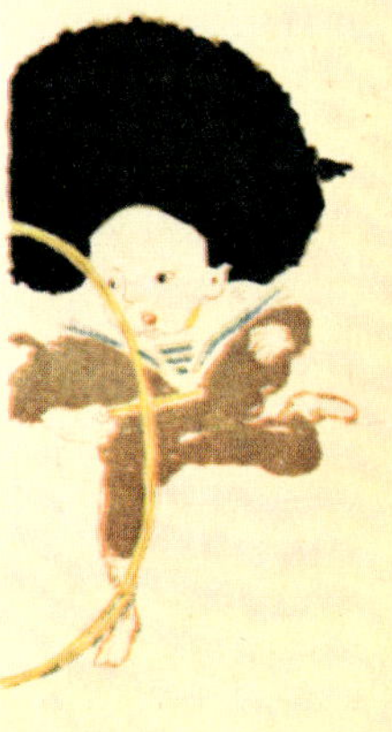

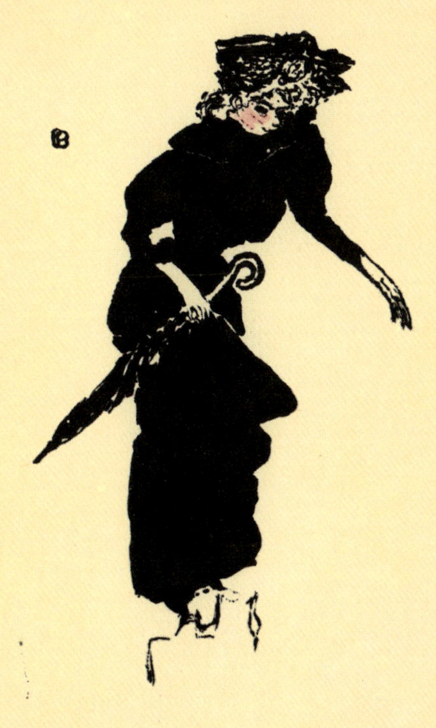

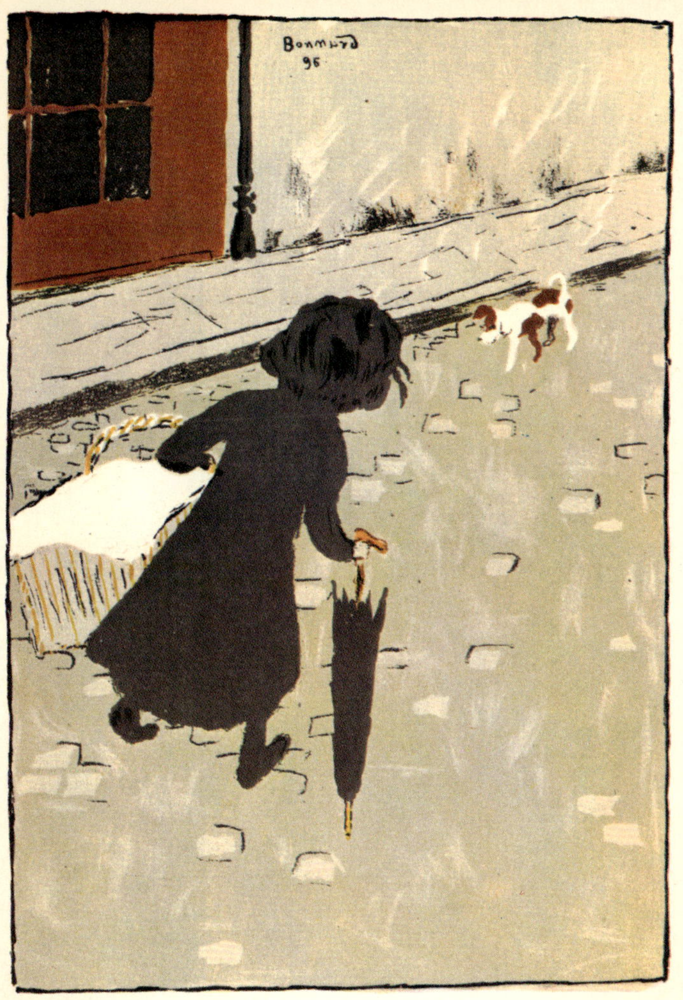
Bonnard
95

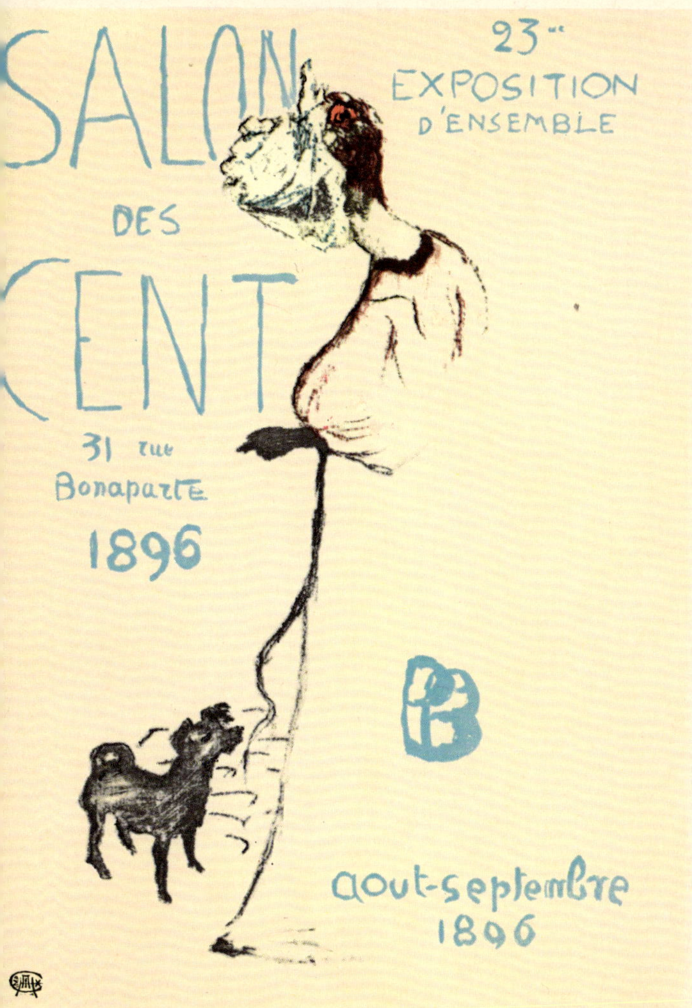

SALON
DES
CENT
31 rue
Bonaparte
1896
23e
EXPOSITION
D'ENSEMBLE
aout-septembre
1896

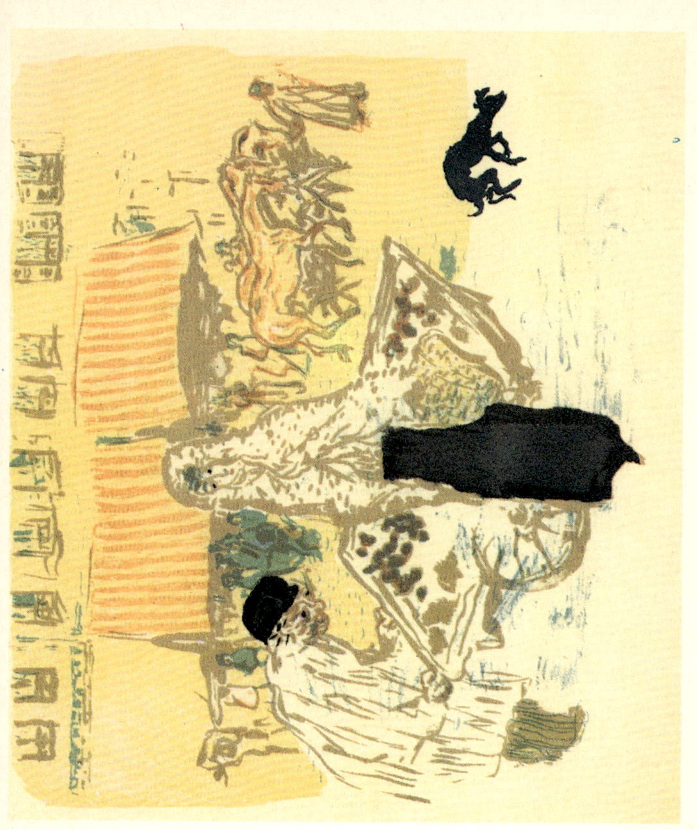

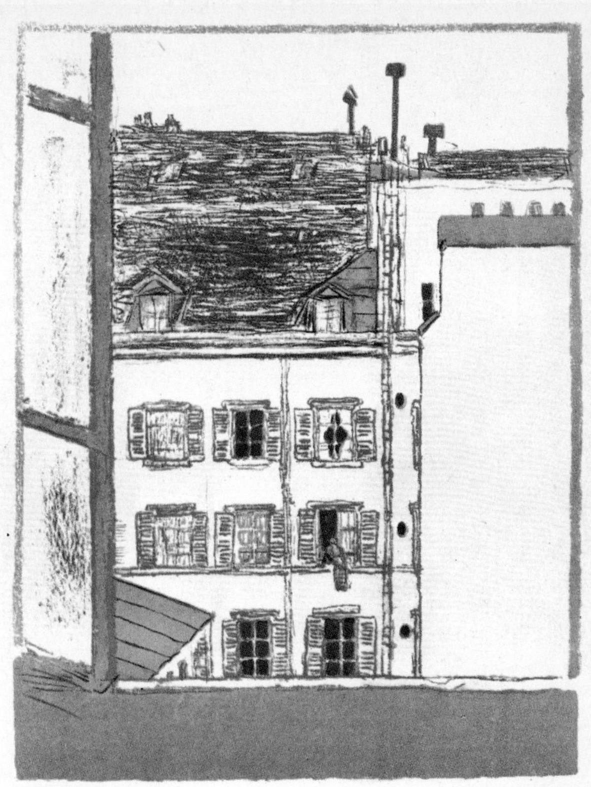

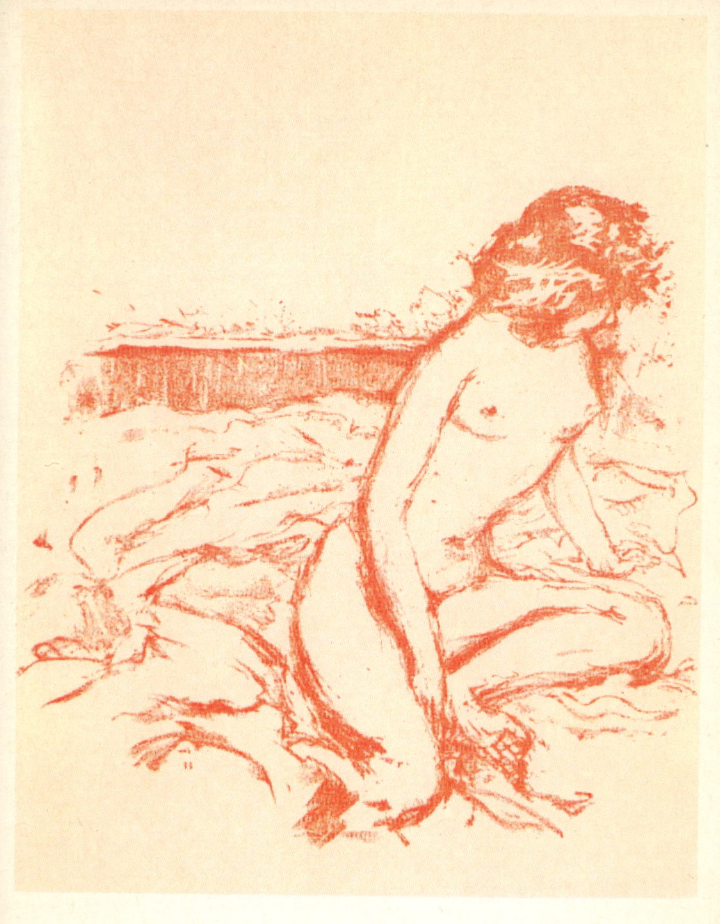

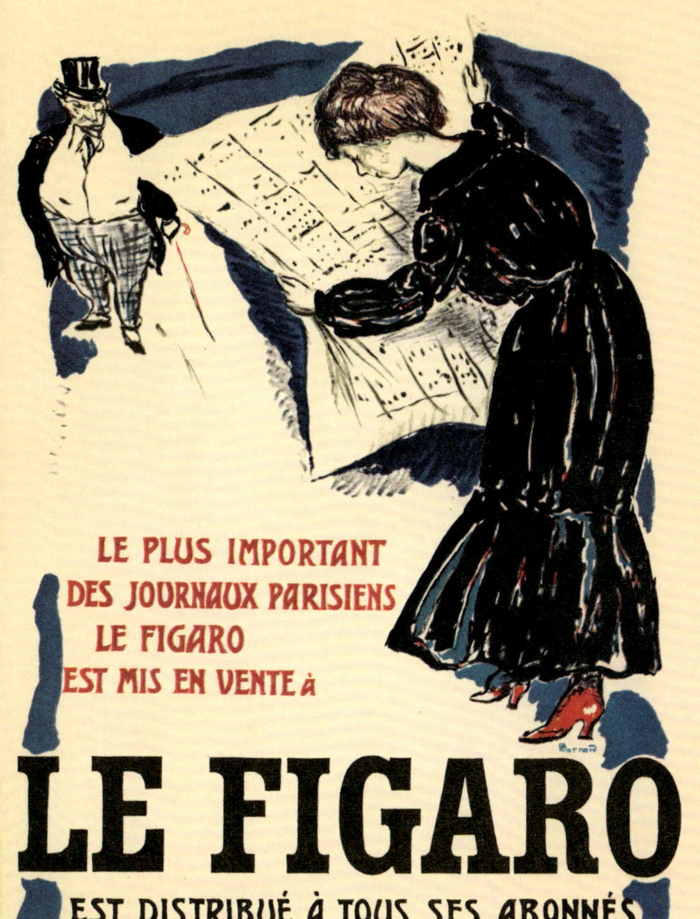

LE PLUS IMPORTANT
DES JOURNAUX PARISIENS
LE FIGARO
EST MIS EN VENTE à
LE FIGARO
EST DISTRIBUÉ À TOUS SES ABONNÉS
AVANT

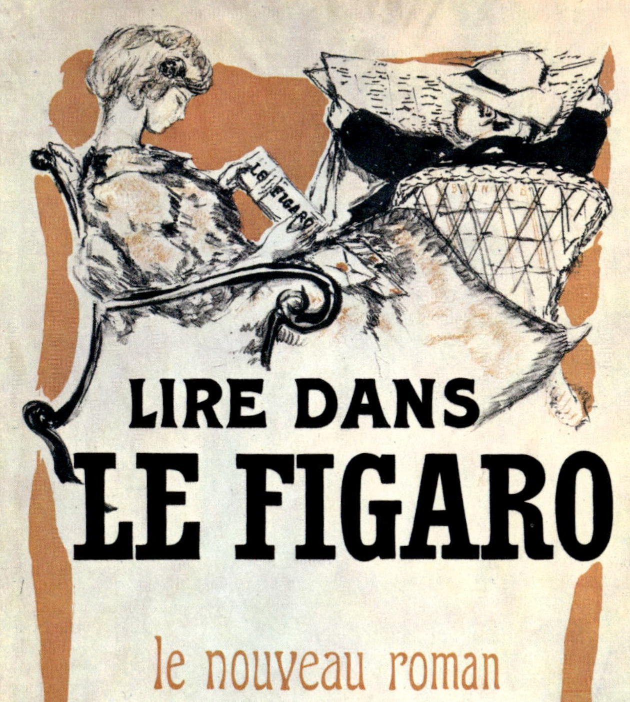

LIRE DANS
LE FIGARO
le nouveau roman
d'Abel HERMANT
Confession d'un Homme d'aujourd'hui
LE FIGARO
AFFICHE D'INTÉRIEUR
IMP. CHAIX, rue Bergère, 20, Paris.

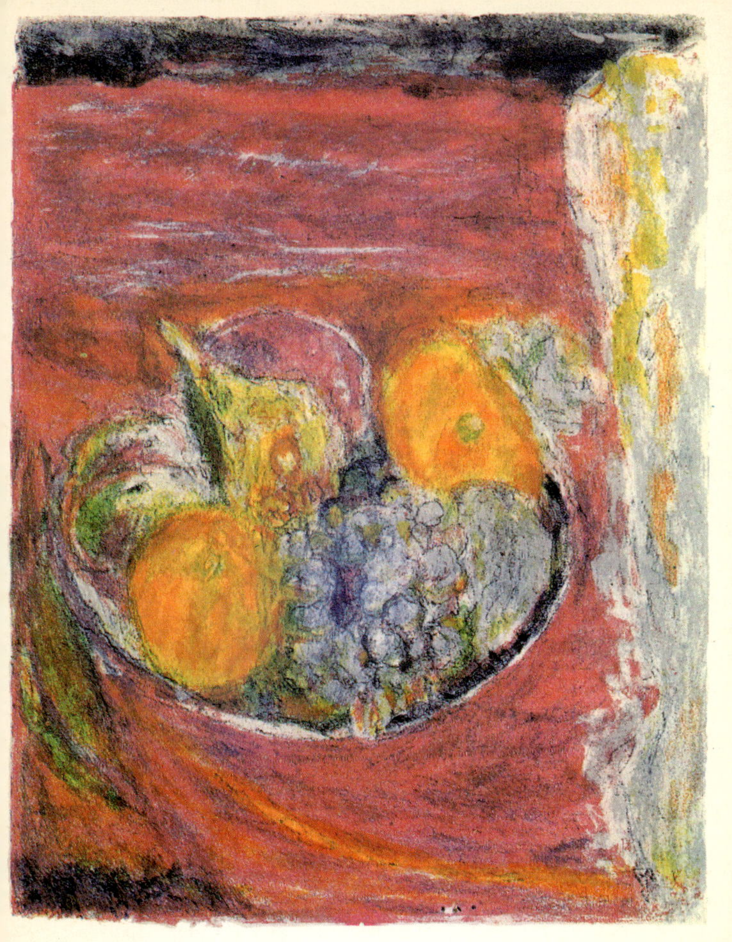

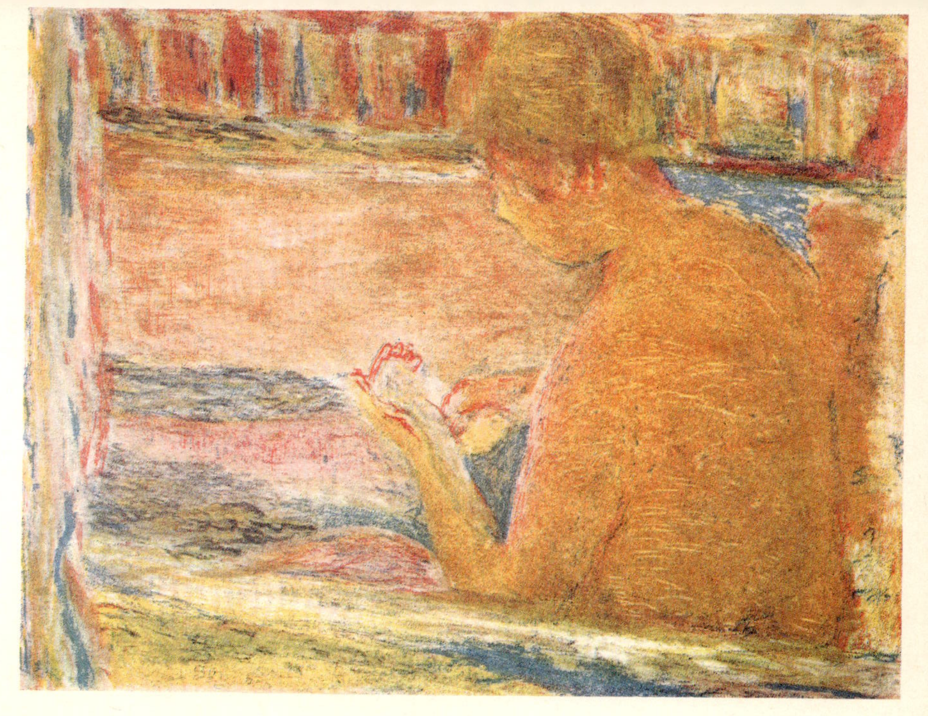